1

# READY TO WRITE

## A FIRST COMPOSITION TEXT

THIRD EDITION

KAREN BLANCHARD • CHRISTINE ROOT

## ANSWER KEY

**Ready to Write 1: A First Composition Text, Third Edition**
**Answer Key**



Pearson Education, 10 Bank Street, White Plains, NY 10606

**Staff credits:** The people who made up the ***Ready to Write 1: A First Composition Text Answer Key*** team, representing editorial, production, design, and manufacturing, are Pietro Alongi, Nancy Flaggman, Christopher Leonowicz, Amy McCormick, Massimo Rubini, Barbara Sabella, Mairead Stack, Jennifer Stem, and Paula Van Ells.

**Text composition:** TSI Graphics
**Text font:** 10/12 Times

ISBN-13: 978-0-13-136331-1
ISBN-10: 0-13-136331-X



Printed in the United States of America
3 4 5 6 7 8 9 10 V036 14 13 12 11 10

# CONTENTS

## CHAPTER 1
# Writing About Yourself

## Grammar Guide: Simple Sentences *(pages 3–4)*

**B.**

2. **subject:** Chris **verb:** kicked **object:** the soccer ball
3. **subject:** She **verb:** is **complement:** shy
4. **subject:** Andrea and Marshall **verb:** ride **object:** bikes
5. **subject:** He **verb:** is **complement:** a banker
6. **subject:** We **verb:** are watching **object:** a movie
7. **subject:** They **verb:** are **complement:** funny
8. **subject:** Leo **verb:** wrote **object:** a paragraph
9. **subject:** Mr. Yang **verb:** is painting **object:** a picture
10. **subject:** I **verb:** bought **object:** a hat

**C.**

1. am
2. are
3. is
4. is
5. are
6. are

**D.**

1. I
2. She, He
3. You, We, They

## Grammar Guide: Capital Letters
*(pages 6–7)*

**B.**

1. I like to travel.
2. Yumi lives in Tokyo, Japan.
3. When did they get back from Mexico?
4. Mr. Kim has a meeting on Friday.
5. Ali is studying Spanish and English this semester.
6. My birthday is in July.
7. What do you want to do on Sunday?
8. Let's meet Julio for lunch on Wednesday.
9. Did you see Mrs. Kara in the library?

## What Is a Paragraph? *(page 8)*

**C.** My name is Ellen Lang. I am twenty-eight years old. I am from Atlanta, Georgia. My native language is English. I am a chef. I work at a restaurant called Noodles. Of course, I like to cook. I also like to play the piano and go out with my friends.

## CHAPTER 2
# Writing About Your Family And Friends

## Writing About Family *(pages 14–16)*

**A.**

1. Sam Simmons and Evelyn Rubin Simmons are Matthew's parents.
2. Alan Simmons and Steve Berger are Matthew's uncles.
3. Martina Geller Simmons and Connie Rubin Berger are Matthew's aunts.
4. Greg Simmons is Matthew's brother.
5. Chris Simmons, Melissa Simmons, Andrea Berger, and Edward Berger are Matthew's cousins.
6. Harriet Simmons and Tammy Rubin are Matthew's grandmothers.
7. Owen Strait is Matthew's nephew.

**B.**

| MALE | FEMALE | MALE OR FEMALE |
|---|---|---|
| brother | daughter | child/children |
| father | aunt | cousin |
| grandfather | granddaughter | parents |
| grandson | grandmother | relative |
| husband | mother | sibling |
| nephew | niece | |
| son | sister | |
| stepfather | stepsister | |
| | wife | |

### Paragraph Pointer: Titles *(page 16)*

1. My Favorite Hobby
2. Our New Neighbor
3. Free-time Is Fun-time
4. Spending Time with Friends
5. Fun in the Sun

## Grammar Guide: Pronouns
*(pages 17–18)*

**Subject Pronouns**

**B.**

1. She
2. It
3. We
4. They
5. He

**Object Pronouns**

**B.**

1. him
2. her
3. him
4. it
5. them
6. me
7. him

**C.**

1. It
2. she
3. She
4. them
5. They
6. I
7. they
8. me
9. she

## Grammar Guide: Possessive Adjectives *(pages 18–19)*

**B.**

1. my
2. her
3. their
4. his
5. their
6. her

**C.**

1. my
2. his
3. His
4. Her
5. my
6. Her

## Grammar Guide: *And, But* *(page 22)*

**B.**

1. Sandra goes out with her cousins, but she goes out with her friends, too.
2. Maria would like to spend more time with her sisters, but she is usually too busy.
3. Erin wants to e-mail her mother, but her computer is broken.
4. Min sent in her application, and she is waiting for the result.
5. My aunt is from Turkey, and my uncle is from Turkey, too.

**D.** My best friend's name is José. He is very responsible, (and) he is also fun to be with. We have a great time whenever we get together. He is smart, (and) he reads a lot. That's why he always has interesting things to say. He is quite a talkative guy, (but) he is a very good listener, too. I can talk about my problems with him, (and) he always gives me good advice. I am really glad to have a friend like José.

# CHAPTER 3
# Writing About Your Activities

## Writing About Activities You Like

*(pages 28–29)*

**A.**

1. play soccer
2. go out to dinner
3. go to movies
4. go to concerts
5. play video games

**C.**

1. Eric likes to do things with his friends in his free time.
2. Eric and his friends like to play soccer after class.
3. Eric and his friends like to go out to dinner, see a movie, and go to concerts, too.

## Grammar Guide: The Simple Present *(pages 29–30)*

**A.**

1. **subject:** I **verb:** ride
2. **subject:** She **verb:** plants
3. **subject:** It **verb:** snows
4. **subject:** They **verb:** watch
5. **subject:** We **verb:** play
6. **subject:** Pam and Lisa **verb:** eat
7. **subject:** He **verb:** collects
8. **subject:** You **verb:** play
9. **subject:** Chris **verb:** listens

**B.** I, They, We, You, Pam and Lisa

**C.** He, She, It, Chris

**D.**

1. he, she, it, or a singular noun.
2. they, we, you, or plural nouns.

**Forming the Simple Present** *(pages 30–31)*

**B.**

a. am
b. are
c. is
d. is
e. is
f. is
g. is
h. are
i. are
j. are
k. are

1. I
2. He, Sam, She, window, It (singular noun)
3. You, We, They, Jane and Chris

**C.**

a. have
b. have
c. has
d. has
e. has
f. has
g. has
h. have
i. have
j. have
k. have

1. he, Isabelle (singular noun), she, book, or it.
2. I, you, we, they, or Lance and Robin (plural nouns).

**Forming Negatives** *(pages 31–32)*

**B.** In his free time, Eric likes to do things with his friends. He often plays soccer with his friends after class. On the weekends, he likes to go out to dinner or go see a movie with them. Eric and his friends go to concerts, too. Sometimes they don't go anywhere, but they aren't bored. They play video games, or they just sit around and talk and laugh. Eric always has fun when he is with his friends.

**C.**

1. Maria **doesn't** worry about her children.
2. We **play** soccer on the weekend.
3. You **are** never on time.
4. She **washes** her clothes every week.
5. Both of my sisters **live** in Texas.
6. I **have** lots of new friends in my class.
7. I **don't** think he watches too much TV.
8. She **has** a lot of friends.
9. He **doesn't** like coffee.
10. They **don't** have a big house.

**D.** **Shelly** likes to spend **her** free time outdoors. **Her** favorite activity is gardening, and **she loves** to plant new kinds of flowers in **her** garden every year. **She** also **enjoys** taking long walks in the park and riding **her** bike. On sunny days, **she goes** to the beach with **her** friends. As you can see, **she loves** being outside in **her** free time.

## Parts of a Paragraph *(pages 33–34)*

1.
   a. I love to play games.
   b. 5
   c. All in all, I think games are fun and challenging.

2.
   a. I have several hobbies that keep me busy in my free time.
   b. 4
   c. In conclusion, my life would not be as much fun without my hobbies.

3.
   a. I live in a big city, so there are many things to do in my free time.
   b. 4
   c. With so many choices, I often have a hard time deciding what to do in my free time.

## Writing About Staying Healthy

*(pages 37–38)*

**B.**

1. eats nutritious foods
2. rides her bike
3. gets checkups
4. gets eight hours of sleep
5. works out
6. does yoga

**C.** I do several things to stay healthy. First of all, I (exercise) regularly. I (work) out at the gym four times a week. I also (ride) my bike to school and (play) tennis on the weekends. In addition, I (am) careful about my diet. For example, I (eat) lots of fruits and vegetables, and I (avoid) junk food. I also (try) to get eight hours of sleep every night. Most importantly, I (quit) smoking! Like many of my friends, staying healthy (is) important to me.

CHAPTER 4

# Giving Instructions

## Writing About How to Make or Do Something *(page 42)*

| | |
|---|---|
| 1. b | 4. c |
| 2. d | 5. f |
| 3. a | 6. e |

## Grammar Guide: Count Nouns and Noncount Nouns

**Count Nouns** *(pages 43–44)*

**A.**

| | |
|---|---|
| 1. an | 5. an, an |
| 2. a | 6. a |
| 3. an | 7. an |
| 4. a | 8. a, an |

**D.**

2. strawberries
3. potatoes
4. loaves
5. knives, children
6. teeth

**Noncount Nouns** *(page 45)*

**B.**

1. I am studying chemistry.
2. I bought some new furniture.
3. I did my homework last night.
4. Correct
5. Do you have information about the movie?
6. The baby drinks a lot of milk every day.

## Time Order Signal Words

*(pages 46–47)*

**B.** "Licking your paws is just the first step. After that, you need to use a good antibacterial body wash, then an exfoliating herbal facial scrub, followed by avocado moisturizing cleanser. . . . "

**C.** Answers may vary. Possible answers:

1. First, Then, Finally
2. First of all, Next, Finally
3. First, Second, Then, Finally

## Grammar Guide: Imperative Sentences *(pages 48–49)*

**B.**

1. get, set, drink, drink, move, Walk, do, keep, take, Eat, go
2. take, let, put, Bring, Turn off, cover, put, Let

**Activity 1** *(pages 48–49)*

**A.** 2 5
3 4
1

**B.** First, put a paper towel under the stain. Then spray the stain with hair spray. After that, rub the stain gently with a clean cloth. Continue rubbing until the stain is completely gone. Finally, wash the piece of clothing as usual.

**Activity 2** *(pages 49–50)*

**A.** 2, 4, 5, 3, 1

**B.** First, loosen the clothing around your neck. Put a cotton pad in the bleeding nostril. Then, sit down with your head leaning forward. Squeeze your nose until it stops bleeding. If your nose continues to bleed, call a doctor.

**Activity 3** *(pages 50–51)*

**A.** 4, 6, 7, 1, 5, 2, 3

**B.** First, you need to make a lid. To do this, draw a circle about 6 inches in diameter on top of the pumpkin around the stem. Then, use a large, sharp knife to cut around the circle and remove the lid. After that, scoop out the seeds and pulp from inside the pumpkin with a large spoon. Next, draw a pattern for the face on the pumpkin with a felt-tip pen. Use a smaller knife to carefully carve out the face you drew on your pumpkin. Then, gently push out the cut-out features to the inside of the pumpkin. Finally, place a small candle inside the pumpkin.

**CHAPTER 5**

# Writing About Your Day

## Writing About a Typical Day

*(pages 56–57)*

**A.**

| | |
|---|---|
| 1. b | 5. e |
| 2. d | 6. h |
| 3. a | 7. g |
| 4. f | 8. c |

## Grammar Guide: Prepositions of Time *(page 58)*

**B.**

| | |
|---|---|
| 1. on | 6. for |
| 2. on | 7. at |
| 3. at | 8. from, to |
| 4. in | 9. in |
| 5. on | 10. at, in |

**C.**

at, from, to, in, from, to, At, for

## Grammar Guide: Frequency Adverbs *(page 60)*

**B.** Dr. Gary Lesneski is an obstetrician. An obstetrician is a doctor who delivers babies. Dr. Lesneski usually gets up at six thirty in the morning. He goes to his office at seven o'clock. His workdays are never typical, but they are always busy. He never knows what time a baby will be born. Sometimes babies are born in the afternoon. Sometimes they are born at night. Often he has to go to the hospital in the middle of the night. He rarely sleeps through an entire night without any interruptions. Dr. Lesneski loves his work, but he looks forward to his vacation in August.

## Grammar Guide: *Before* and *After*

*(pages 61–62)*

**B.**

1. Before I eat dinner, I wash my hands. *or* I wash my hands before I eat dinner.
2. Before I watch TV, I do my homework. *or* I do my homework before I watch TV.
3. Before I do my homework, I go to the gym. *or* I go to the gym before I do my homework.
4. Before I eat breakfast, I read the newspaper. *or* I read the newspaper before I eat breakfast.

**C.**

1. After I get home from school, I take my dog for a walk. *or* I take my dog for a walk after I get home from school.
2. After I eat dinner, I wash the dishes. *or* I wash the dishes after I eat dinner.
3. After I get to school, I have coffee with my friends. *or* I have coffee with my friends after I get to school.
4. After I read my son a story, I put him to bed. *or* I put my son to bed after I read him a story.

**E.** "On Mondays, I <u>get</u> ready to plan my week. On Tuesdays, I <u>plan</u> my week. On Wednesdays, I <u>revise</u> my plan for the week. On Thursdays, I <u>put</u> my plan for the week into my computer. On Fridays, I <u>think</u> about starting my plan for next week."

### Paragraph Pointer: Paragraph Unity

*(page 63)*

**A.** During the week, my days are boring.

**B.**

1. I have two younger sisters.
2. Ben also works at the library.

### Paragraph Pointer: Time Order

*(pages 64–65)*

**B.**

1. 1, TS, 2, 3, 4
2. 2, TS, 3, 1, 4
3. 1, 3, 2, TS, 4

**C.**

1. I am usually very lazy on Sundays.
2. I get up late, and I eat a big breakfast; After breakfast, I read the newspaper for a few hours; Sometimes I talk to my friends on the telephone; At four o'clock, I am usually hungry, so I make a snack. Then I watch TV or take a nap; In the evening, I often go out to dinner with my friends, but I am back in bed again at ten o'clock.
3. I like to relax on Sunday so that I am ready to start my week on Monday.

**D.** **Paulo is** usually very lazy on Sundays. **He gets** up late, and **he eats** a big breakfast. After breakfast, **he reads** the newspaper for a few hours. Sometimes **he talks** to **his** friends on the telephone. At four o'clock, **he is** usually hungry, so **he makes** a snack. Then **he watches** TV or **takes** a nap. In the evening, **he** often **goes to** dinner with **his** friends, but **he is** back in bed again at ten o'clock. **He likes** to relax on Sunday so that **he is** ready to start **his** week on Monday.

**CHAPTER 6**

# Writing Descriptions

## Describing People *(pages 73–74)*

**A.**

1. a
2. d
3. b
4. c
5. e

**B.** Answers will vary. Possible answers:

1. Dino has long, dark hair and a mustache. He is short and stocky. He has a mole on his cheek. Today he is wearing jeans with a turtleneck and a sweater. He always has a big smile.
2. Claudia is a tall, slim teenage girl with very long legs. She has wavy red hair and usually wears glasses. Today she is wearing big earrings and tight pants.

## Grammar Guide: Present Progressive *(page 76)*

**C.**

a. is wearing, is carrying, is reading
b. is wearing, is carrying, is talking
c. is wearing, is carrying
d. is wearing, is (also) wearing, is listening
e. is wearing, She's (also) wearing

## Grammar Guide: Adjectives

*(page 78)*

**B.**

a. tall, thin, bald, black, big, blue, striped
b. slender, young, average, long, straight, blond, beautiful, plaid, leather
c. short, young, round, curly, red, big, green, favorite
d. good-looking, average, straight, black, brown, corduroy, new, white
e. attractive, long, wavy, brown, big, beautiful, grey, black, silver, long

**C.** My name is Jenny Marsh. I am tall and thin. I have long black hair and big brown eyes. Today I am wearing old wool pants and a soft yellow sweater. I have on a brown belt and white sneakers.

## Describing a Person's Character

*(page 80)*

1. My roommate Akiko is a very organized person.
2. For example, all of her clothes are arranged by color, and her shoes her neatly arranged on the shelf; Her books are arranged by topic; She keeps her CDs in her bookcase in alphabetical order so they are always easy to find; She puts all of her important papers in a file in the top drawer so nothing ever gets lost.

### Paragraph Pointer: Examples *(page 80)*

Answers will vary. Possible answers:

1. she reads and studies for hours on weekends.
2. she is a volunteer tutor of English to new immigrants.
3. he yells if anyone steps on his lawn.
4. he makes the most incredibly silly faces when he has to eat something he doesn't like.

## Describing Things *(pages 84–85)*

**A.**

1. candlesticks
2. flowered plate
3. Chinese rug
4. Turkish towels
5. leather gloves

**B.**

1. wooden, hand-carved, perfect, beautiful
2. round, hand-painted, colorful, bright, nice
3. rectangular, silk, wool, geometric, Chinese, beautiful
4. plush, Turkish, large, soft, blue, white, green, white
5. brown, leather, soft, smooth, attractive

**CHAPTER 7**

# Writing About Places

## Describing a Room *(pages 93–95)*

**A.** My bedroom is small and cozy. There are two big windows on the back wall, so my room is usually bright and sunny. On the left wall, I have a wooden desk with three drawers where I do my homework. All of my books are in a bookcase next to the desk. My bed is on the right wall. There is a painting of a bowl of fruit and flowers above my bed. I love the bright colors of the flowers. I also have a large dresser next to my bed. There are several photographs of my family on top of it and a square mirror above it. Finally, there is a green and white oval rug in front of the dresser. I enjoy spending time in my bedroom.

**B.** Answers will vary. Possible answers:

**Room 1:** books, bulletin board, closet, dresser, hockey stick, lamp, nightstand, painting, poster
**Room 2:** bedspread, chair, computer, curtains, desk, dresser, mirror, nightstand, lamp, poster, rug, tennis racquet, wastebasket
**Room 3:** alarm clock, bedspread, blinds, books, chair, closet, fan, ice skates, lamp, nightstand, plant, poster, TV

**C.** Answers will vary. Possible answers:

**Room 1:** messy, cluttered, small
**Room 2:** clean, neat, orderly, sunny
**Room 3:** cozy, comfortable, neat, orderly

## Grammar Guide: *There is* and *There are* *(page 96)*

**B.** My bedroom is small and cozy. There are two big windows on the back wall, so my room is usually bright and sunny. On the left wall, I have a wooden desk with three drawers where I do my homework. All of my books are in a bookcase next to the desk. My bed is on the right wall. There is a painting of a bowl of fruit and flowers above my bed. I love the bright colors of the flowers. I also have a large dresser next to my bed. There are several photographs of my family on top of it and a square mirror above it. Finally, there is a green and white oval rug in front of the dresser. I enjoy spending time in my bedroom.

## Grammar Guide: Prepositions of Place *(pages 96–97)*

**B.**

1. above, in front of, in, on, next to (*or* beside)
2. in, on, between, on, under

**CHAPTER 8**

# Writing A Narrative

## Writing a Story *(page 108)*

**B.**

3 1 4
2 6 5

## Grammar Guide: Simple Past

*(pages 110–111)*

**E.** had, was, got, pushed, stopped, got, pushed, closed, started, stopped, felt, looked, began, was, opened, were, was, had, called, waited, felt, brought, climbed, was

**F.** I had a busy day yesterday. I woke up at 7:00 A.M. and got dressed. Then, I ate breakfast, read the paper, and checked my e-mail. After that, I took the bus to school and went to classes from 10:00 A.M. to 4:00 P. M. Next, I studied for a few hours at the library before I had a quick dinner and went to work at the bookstore on campus. At 9:30 P.M., my friend drove me home. When I got home, I watched the news on TV and went to sleep.

**G.** invented, were, moved, gave, loved, continued, graduated, went, was, taught, loved, studied, earned, went, met, became, wrote, created, called, grew, became, was, started, made

## Writing Narrative Paragraphs

**Activity 1** *(page 112)*

**A.**

2 4
1 3

**B.** Answers will vary. Possible answers:

**Picture 1:** Bob and Sally went out to dinner. They ordered an expensive meal.
**Picture 2:** The meal tasted delicious. They were happy.
**Picture 3:** Bob got the bill. He looked for his wallet, but it was not in his jacket.
**Picture 4:** Bob and Sally had to wash dishes to pay for their meal. They were tired and embarrassed.

**Activity 2** *(pages 113–115)*

1. 3, 2, 5, 1, 4
2. 3, 6, 1, 2, 4, 7, 5
3. 4, 1, 3, 2, 8, 6, 5, 7
4. 2, 4, 1, 3, 5, 8, 6, 7

**CHAPTER 9**

# Expressing Your Opinion

## What Do You Think? *(pages 130–132)*

**A.**

1. airport
2. stadium
3. park
4. office
5. restaurant
6. taxi
7. hotel room
8. train
9. movie theater
10. shopping mall
11. auditorium
12. bus stop

**C.**

1. a. There should be a ban on smoking in public places.
   b. Nonsmokers have a right to clean air; Cigarette smoke is disgusting and dangerous; Smoking is bad for the health of smokers; Banning will help smokers quit smoking.
2. a. It is unfair to ban smoking in public places.
   b. Nonsmokers should not have more rights than smokers; If nonsmokers don't want to be in a smoke-filled room, they can go somewhere else; Smoking is a legal activity; The government shouldn't say that a legal activity is illegal in some places.

### Paragraph Pointer: Order of Importance *(pages 134–135)*

**B.**

Answers may vary. Possible answers:

1. First of all, In addition, Most importantly
2. For one thing, Also, Finally

## Writing About Inventions

### Prewriting *(page 139)*

**A.**

1. TV
2. light bulb
3. telescope
4. computer
5. penicillin
6. printing press
7. telephone
8. car
9. airplane